INTERLUDE

LJ IRETON

HAYWOOD BOOKS

HAYWOOD BOOKS
an imprint of Renard Press Ltd
124 City Road, London EC1V 2NX
United Kingdom

info@renardpress.com
020 8050 2928
www.haywoodbooks.com

Interlude first published by Haywood Books in 2025

Text © LJ Ireton, 2025

Cover design by Will Dady

Printed on FSC-accredited papers in the UK by 4edge Limited

ISBN: 978-1-80447-153-1

9 8 7 6 5 4 3 2 1

LJ Ireton asserts her moral right to be identified as the author of this work in accordance with the Copyright, Designs and Patents Act 1988.

These poems are a work of fiction. Any resemblance to actual persons, living or dead, is purely coincidental, or is used fictitiously.

CLIMATE POSITIVE   Renard Press is proud to be a climate positive publisher, removing more carbon from the air than we emit and planting a small forest. For more information see renardpress.com/eco.

All rights reserved. This publication may not be reproduced, stored in a retrieval system or transmitted, in any form or by any means – electronic, mechanical, photocopying, recording or otherwise – without the prior permission of the publisher.

EU Authorised Representative: Easy Access System Europe
Mustamäe tee 50, 10621 Tallinn, Estonia, gpsr.requests@easproject.com.

Contents

Interlude

The moon and black sun	3
A September gloaming	4
An equinox	5
Birdsong	6
The unspoken	7
The silence of the birds	8
The gratitude of flowers	9
Hungry	10
Facing November	11
Sunflowers at sunset	12
Still	13
This cobalt morning	14
After the rain	15
White horses	16
The colour purple	17
Ducklings	18
The swallows	19
Pied wagtail minute	20
Sea words at dawn	21
Summoning waves	22
Sixty signatures	23
Turning into dark	24
A break in the rain	25
Two birds	26
The other world	27

The soul knows how   28
Some days…   29
Two sides of the window   30
The peace prize   31
A restless heart   32
Dark horses   33
Imaginations   34
Foragers   35
Winter clouds   36
On snow and flame   37
All things descending   38
When wintering is done   39
Interlude   40
A waiting season   41
Not yet spring   42
The Aldgate horses   44
The Boleyn haunting   45
Night writing   47
Shepherdess   48
The still morning   49
Acknowledgements   50
About the poet   52

INTERLUDE

To my angels with claws

The moon and black sun

In the blue morning,
the moon lingers –
a midnight chalk white
spirit
insists

and sits above my sunflower,
black like charcoal
simmering in a fire petal pit –
red embers
at the tilt of its face.

They look at each other –
rebellious discs
still
in conjunction
with light and dark.

They are in this together –
eclipsing my expectations
of day, of flower –

a glowing ghost
and burning cloak,
both
where I looked for sun.

A September gloaming

The flower suns have fallen,
releasing small sleeping stars
encased in beetle shells
into my hands.
I sit, pensive
looking at where the high petals were –
their gold-pink now given to
gloaming September skies,
the blood blush in the cold.
Maybe nothing goes,
but is in another place to find
as the world turns.
Still, it is harder to see in the dark,
and I prefer to be barefoot
with the transient flowers at twilight.

An equinox

It was an equinox –
a mourning –
I stroked the shell of a horse chestnut seed
with my thumb
and crows cawed under
grey clouds neon –
causing the sun to tumble out
as if confused from sleep;
burning on instinct –
unsure who had summoned,
but eager to answer.
And even with my face to the fire,
remembering,
a cold future snaked along my skin –
because all is in-between,
isn't it?
Ever moving,
we long for one star or another,
with reverie or inertia,
lacking the steadiness of birdsong,
of singing, whatever the sky.

Birdsong

There is a tint this evening.
The robin sings in pink and grey
even if no one hears him,
like the birdsong gone before, forgotten.
I can dwell on reason so much
that nothing gets written at all,
but the twilight tonight is lighter;
a smoky rose
and my words begin on the branches,
breathed out into the cloud lines
pink and grey.
Maybe they won't be heard,
but it's about the saying –
back into the sky
living, before the night.

The unspoken

In the quiet in-between –
liquid mirror purple dark,
the spirit of the sun
lingers
like perfume the fox cubs sniff and pounce,
while the adults wait for the moon;
heady, expectant –
for truths drawn out and
dreams pinned under the heavy sun
to crawl silver
from the earth.

It is the time of the crepuscular,
the knowing –
follow the cats, they sense the turning
in this grey,
when vision of your hands fades
but the unspoken is growing,
black rose word petals appear –
the lines of poetry breathe
with the breath of nocturnal creatures
raising their heads.

The silence of the birds

In the inhale of the earth,
the silence of the birds,
the watching for the white sun –
dry words are breathing.

When the wind has torn the forests,
but the moorhens deem it safe
to walk on dirty water –
write of their returning.

When the tree arms unbend
and creatures crawl curious,
unsinging,
there is the poem;
the tin-grey cloud in its palm –
eyes towards its absence.

The gratitude of flowers

I want to stay here under the gratitude
of flowers –
my hair tangled and dangling
in the breeze
like the leaf tips
and long grass,
like the reeds.

I have tried to replicate petals
in otherwise plain places –
where closed hearts choose
symbols
over creativity,
white over green,
the loneliness of lines
where wings aren't welcome.

Do you give any minute,
wherever you are,
to the wildflowers red,
the side-eyed look
of the bird?

Someone
put flowers on your table today
and you walk past
without a word.

Hungry

The falling sun and an unformed poem
were hungry for my attention.
I stood in-between them,
on a balcony
both could reach,
and with creation's infinite alchemy
fed them to each other.

Facing November

The clouds are giant gull's wings
swept back, rows of flight
all turned towards
the low sun,
hung with lace herself.
She wants you to believe
in the folklore of
naked skin
under the sky,
for your wishes
to sustain her
under the veil;
feather-sweet as imaginary birds,
rolling need into the burn.

Sunflowers at sunset

I shivered on a summer evening;
gold, rose, grey sky,
in my T-shirt –
the sunflowers at sunset
before me dancers bowing
at the end of the song.

The blood rush is banished
to memories
now –
a ride home recalling
fingertips
and skin

before the cold blast
of late-night air
turns your head,
ruins everything.

Still

Thyme touched my fingertips
as I cut the dry stalks,
crushed the lavender into my thoughts
and turned the soil over –
it is still hot for September.

The dill flowers float like open umbrellas
into gold that's not a memory yet,
coriander clusters like witch circles of insect wings –
still wishing.

Scents linger on my skin,
on the clipped air –
invisible living colours
that reach into my summer-scared soul
and say *it is still here* –
like the cabbage white did for one curious minute this morning.
Did it know how much I needed that touch on my shoulder?

On my knees
I sweep up the dried twigs and my belief
that my time outside was finished
with the fade of purple,
the appearance of cobwebs in the herbs.

This cobalt morning

In the darkest time,
under the mid-season blue sky,
I find each robin by their song,
heralding me into this
cobalt morning
from three trees –
an open-beaked tryptich.
Everything about me is reluctant.
Everything about you
beckons
the whole cold earth
to come and turn under your tiny feet.
And I do –
walk under the
exhaling,
heat-coloured hearts
of winter.

After the rain

Out of the mud marshes of Middle England,
rainbows rise wide and down.
At their source, molten silver has pooled
around mounds of stubborn grass,
making the brown sludge beautiful
and white birds, not minding the shallow,
sit on the sheen,
dotting the water under the distanced trees
and tantrum-tired sky.
The spectrum draws eyes over the sodden
landscape, the leaden background –
but the gulls only look forward,
resting on the reflected light,
making fields the sea.

White horses

The reflection of the snow-feathered egret
under the willow,
wings wide on the water,

the sight of white horses,
walking celestial,
nodding moonlight in the field –

the sky guides us
to the old earth,
the new.

Amongst the dust, the crumbling, the ash,
stars fly in the river,
faith chews on fading grass.

The colour purple

The meadowsweet is a sparkling mist ring
around the dark water.
The grasses are tall, their tops
spun with field colours;
flaxen, corn.

But only one shade appears in the pool;
the purple spires of loosestrife –
striking unearthly indigo
reflections before my eyes.

I step back
and all the violet steps forward –
for a moment I am twelve,
reading a text about
God wanting
the colour purple
to impress.

I notice you now, blood-willow flowers,
bowing to your own selves –
wine seeping into my consciousness.

And decades-old words
on a yellowing page,
waiting across the cream fields of time –
it turns out they were purple, too.

Ducklings

It's a transformation;
losing something human –
to kiss cold lake
water lilies
under rain clouds.

Only then are you allowed
to breathe in their time –
the tiniest
all fur, flower-head ducklings
discovering how to survive,
where water changes to leaf
underneath their feet.

You must give up your ground
to see prayers of the pond
standing.

The swallows

The swallows glide in a line;
symbols pass the clouds behind –
they leap like heartbeats on a screen,
tiny
pulses of life.

Pied wagtail minute

One pause in the rain
incessant –
I breathe in the after air,
watch two wagtails hoop a bow
over the water.
This moment was theirs to tie
and worth my tread
under
moody, volatile skies.

Sea words at dawn

I miss what the sea would say to me
in the morning –

risen from the seabed,
language untranslated,
sage on the burning surface,
bubbling like sherbet
from touching the sun.

If I walked a while now,
I would find a stream
with teacups' worth of water –
murmuring an inland elegy
filtered through grey cotton
and wrung into a sigh.

It too has a memory
of a song no one composes;
fire-words living on the blue horizon,
spoken wherever it is dawn.

Summoning waves

I thought the sea
seeped in through my ears in sleep
to quench my dreams
with sparkling turquoise salt
liquid.

Every time I missed it.

But those images swim in my water mind;
my blood the tides to the same moon.
Like to like, maybe the waves are
not distinct –
just night calling up my deepest self
to rejoin me
at the surface.

Sixty signatures

I went for the falling sun –
its lullaby wide and wild at the sea's edge,
dark blue pushing pale-yellow light
into conclusion.

But I found rows and rows of seabirds –
yellow beaks, black heads,
brown on white over red
heartbeats,
waiting.

The last dip of the sun was the twilight lift –
one by one, curved grey sketches
grew a feather tip,
blacker and black, flying right into the set –

and sixty signatures were signed above my head.
The wings – so many wings –
inked and seeped into the sunset,
their silhouettes moving
left to right,
writing over a star, the shades of light
sinking
into a forever paper sky.

Turning into dark

I was balancing on one leg,
hands in prayer, focused
under the amaranthine sky.
You were curled around my ankle,
excitable from the evening air.

They appeared then,
bewitching –
a whole flock of pigeons above,
dipping grey practised wings
into the purple line of houses
then tilting back up, on a breath,
a hyphen.

We watched them –
you with round, yellow, reptile eyes,
as close to the birds as I –
prey, multiplied into melted iron shapes,
punctuating the end of a light-pink day.

And now the turning into dark
was made beautiful,
beautiful because it was shared;
us crouched and facing them together,
their own bodies flying close –
all creatures side by side
going into the lavender night.

A break in the rain

A break in the rain
of November –
a family of moorhens
patter up a bank
under the yellow leaves,
ghostly green in the middle
clinging on –
or maybe
a moment of spring
for these brown younglings.
For me,
a kinder cold,
visible soft –
before half a moon
sinks us back into the season
of wishing it still
was.

Two birds

Two birds broke free, sudden
into the blue
from behind continental clouds.

Tiny, tiny, away from
clock-face clutches
and human musts,
they lift my lungs
I've been failing to fill,
as my muscles sink sighing
into the ground –
I can watch them fly.

I can watch them fly
and nothing else.

The other world

I can't describe the mystery of healing –

I only know the feeling
of crying into my cat's fur –
like my own solitary cloud –

and hearing her rolling purr,
like all life is silent
apart from her way of breathing.

That a form of prayer
is listening to the rhythms of the other world –

the angels with claws.

The soul knows how

My cat swirls around the solid floor,
head first, like a slick otter in a stream –
this is how she shows happiness.
We have the words, so many words,
but underneath,
or before,
the soul knows how to dance,
how to purr.

Some days...

It's not even
that you feel heavy –
but there is no flickering flame
reaching out
of you
today
to grab,
to hold,
to burn.

Open the window.
Let the outside trace
your outline
in light blue.
Watch the dust-like rain –
barely visible,
only touching surfaces
with the strength of tears –
absent of its own storm.

Sit with it.

And be tame together.

Two sides of the window

We are perfect stillness –
my two circled cats and I.
Outside, the wind is
crying, chaotic –
a reedy sound slipping
in through the walls
to haunt our contentment –
only for the contrast to enhance it.
I light another candle,
a silent soldier
against the cold,
and I write
about both
needing each other
for a poem.

The peace prize

If I'm quiet now,
on my own a lot,
ink under plants,
tree trunk by water,
it's because
I'm done with chaos.

I've taken my shoes off.

My own mind was
tangled noise –
metal signals, siren doubts,
screaming loud,
loud
for sanity.

Silence
once was to me
an unreachable, precious prayer –
the ghostlike glitter-water imagined by
a thirsting throat
in the desert.

I dipped disbelieving, grateful hands
into this stream.

And here I swim.

Here I swim.

A restless heart

You can hear the wings
of a restless heart –
beat, beat,
beating against
its resistance.
There are no fae-like fluttering dreams
for those whose
imagination never sleeps,
but a weighted emerald bird
with a sharp beak;
always waiting on something
in this slow world –
a heavy hope, creation
hovering
in a ball of energy –
beat, beat,
beating until
you can see
her.

Dark horses

I tried to control chaos with my hands.
It rebelled, rearing up
in swirls and streams of black smoke −
tendril tails escaping through my fingers.

Determined to keep it captured,
I cried in frustration, tears fizzing
crimson blue into the black matter.

Eventually you pried my
despairing, frozen fingers open −
clusters of nightmares and ferocity
floated before us,
buoyant in release.

Together, we watched black holes come and go,
grey-light dust shapes, purple shadows.
Champagne star signs and Stygian dark horses
crossed my palms −
calmer now, curious.

You said:
Some things are not ours to hold.
And I thought −
I would like to write about
dark horses.

Imaginations

I thought wishing
was meant to be weightless –
an entire silver world
existing within a snowflake.
But somehow, carrying
beautiful imaginations
for a long time
only makes them
heavier.

Foragers

The forest floor is awash with dead;
once floated, dried ochre statuettes
of rusting leaves.
But running along the sides,
under the shimmering ivy,
two rats break through
the flat hearts, head first
while squirrels dig for
solid memories from the past.
One robin holds a red berry
like a third eye –
it has plucked blood
from the path of time.
In life's falling hours,
I watch foragers
dive under endings,
black eyes open –
possibility
is a constant.

Winter clouds

I resent the winter mornings
and I am slow to the window.
My arms are closed tight around myself
when I see the rose-golden clouds,
outstretched south and over
my reluctance to stand here.

The cold feels necessary now –
as I take an iron step under the glow
to be part of this pink
conjuring
that I could have missed.

Without seeing the sun
and mourning it even before
November,
it lives on.
It lives on
in these faithful clouds –
they carry
something that is still to come.

On snow and flame

There are dried flowers in the candle white;
purple stars
with faces pressed to the glass,
looking out
at the raining snowflakes –
falling faster than my thoughts
that flurry only.

I focus on the flame,
trying to
mimic its tilting contentment –
but still
my inner wishes circle.

Melting meets melting.
Yet what could be,
what could be –

won't settle.

All things descending

The season falls. I watch,
without control,
the split and bounce of conkers
into the mist,
the rain and covering of burnt orange
shed by the sun.

The wind sweeps time up
in front of me,
sailed on by a yellow wagtail.
She still looks like spring.
But the squirrels are ready –
listening, claws sharp
and eager to dig.

I'm not sure what I'm meant to let go of
or search for
under the wisps of this year,
settling.

Maybe all things descending
will leave answers in my hands –
hopes to paint on pinecones
ideas freed from shells
or the evergreen of the ivy;
forever sure of herself.

When wintering is done

It is a surprising morning –
like the cold is trying to be kind.
The sun hits pink on the grass
sprinkled with ice,
glittering.
But the yellow-bellied bluebird
above me is the future sun –
the creatures all to come out
when wintering is done.
We have other selves,
waiting,
to leave the nest of our senses.
Then, instead, we will see
spirits sparkling,
ours
on the grass.

Interlude

Where are you, robin, in the rain?
Do you know that it is solstice –
that the light is coming?

Are you nestled, knowing only
that is it not time to sing now –
your wings blanket
to some tiny souls,
eyes blinking in the brown night?

I think that you are more patient than I –
and if daybreak is dry
you will sing with the same rhythm of the earth
that you felt
in the wet interlude,
when I was mourning slowness.

And yet your song will be, unmistakably, joy,
as if you were kept back –
and I will understand that.

I will understand that.

A waiting season

There were no birds or
shadows under this nonchalant sky
of October;
I mourned yellow
and beaded eyes on the pond –
the slowness of floating.
I consoled myself
with the rust-painted reeds:
pleasing like red apples on snow,
but these months, I know,
are a waiting for beauty;
thinking of the times I was in the right place,
only later revealing to me why.
In the evening the lead-grey clouds
rolled into a gold wheatfield
falling of a sunset,
twilight burning from the
white unused drift of the day.

Not yet spring

It is not yet spring,
when I can call my curated vines
of violet and lemon meaning
out of the ground
from winter's writhing roots
that press against the edges of my mind
and curl back around
in want of surety,
sun-blessings,
the curiosity of others.

It is not yet spring,
the unravelling of the tangible
into Time,
that doesn't go back again
into the dark –
it dances on your lips,
dips into hedgerows
in pastel colours,
sense-making,
breathing purple.

It is not yet spring,
when I can watch
what I already know

like a kite
tipping its head
at its tail;
streamer roots
tasting the sky.

Not yet.

The Aldgate horses

The stars are on you;
steel sinew and black night.
They saw the russet muscle and mane –
they still do.
Iron shoes hammered under starlight
now cool in the fountain –
a memory of earth water;
squelching feet in fields
with cleaner conscience,
louder heartbeats.
The life of London
was the breath of a horse,
lost, lost
in Tyger-roared smog –
we cough up smoke
under stone readings of oxygen
days, stroke your sculptured face
for a pulse,
touch your bronze nose,
standing stone
for medieval movement –
and run.

The Boleyn haunting

I see, then, that I am to be silenced —

my letters, burnt language, buckles
inwards, inwards into a place
where words don't exist.

Desire can't be undone. But
denial dissipates the bonds
we made of ink crosses on parchment —
dancing black strokes
transfuse
into dust.

And in this new, blue light signing
I am unclaimed.
Under sentences of men,
down through cold century floors,
will memory hold its shape
enough
in the telling
of this?

I imagine a haunting.
Not of revenge —
but a ghosting of truth;

the voice of conscience
is too soul-heavy
to be lost in consciousness.

There I will leave my voice –
waiting beyond speech,
latent and
lingering.

Night writing

I know that to write
I must wait for the Little Bear
to peer through performance curtains,
for the moon to mark a pathway through
the frothing mass of the midnight sea,
for the truth washed up with colourless stones
on a black beach, shadow-hoping for poetry.
Because Night has released black hearts,
sateen wings by the thousands,
that circle the orb sparkling
and swarm to fire, eyes, desk lights and doubts –
flying dust we can't express by day.
There is weight to your words
written in charcoal quiet
that were already there in the falling –
thoughts sifted from perfumed dusk,
falling on to the purple floor of Evensong.

And now you see them –
the gold metal specks on a moth's back –
the stars that burned with intention
to become the patterned constellations
of language
in the dark.

Shepherdess

If I was one of Blake's angels
in the fields at night
on bright feet,
I would stroke a sheep's smooth nose
like I did at a sanctuary
and pray over their fleece –
wiry and woven with dried leaves –
until the death number is mist,
drifting into human dreams.
I would let their horizontal eyes
see into the white heart
I inherited –
let the lamb leap into my ethereal arms
the way innocent stars did
when they were young.
And I would hold him
like he was the lost one,
ask the lion to lie down
and fold my wings, letting the wolves in –
they are not the hunters in this place,
who choose the extinguishing of a soft star
in shadows far and veiled
from sight.

The still morning

It thundered unkind across the island
like a tithe taken in the dark
for seeking sanctuary.

The force was roaring on beauty —
why blow on stone already smooth,
scatter water with water?

Yet the dawn was an empty lung,
a casual sun strolled across the sky,
the stray cats stretched into the light,
unnerved.

Your turn, the towers of palm said,
rustle-less,
to leave your questions with the storm,
the thoughts that bite each other.

A white dove flew from a terracotta roof,
the sky a fire blue;
neither were thinking about rain.

Acknowledgements

'Dark horses' first published in *Mausoleum Press* in June 2022.

'The unspoken' first published in *Hog Literary Magazine* in December 2023.

'Turning into dark' first published in *Spelt Magazine* in April 2024.

'All things descending' first published in *Green Ink Poetry* in December 2023.

'The Aldgate horses' published in *Spellbinder Literary Journal* in January 2024.

'Interlude' first published in *Wild Greens* in February 2024.

'The Boleyn haunting' first published in *York Literary Review* in 2023.

A NOTE ON SUSTAINABILITY

We feel strongly that there is no denying the climate crisis, and we all have a part to play in fixing the problem.

As an imprint of Renard Press, we are proud to be one of the UK's first climate-positive publishers, taking more carbon out of the air than we put in. How? We reduce our emissions as much as possible, using green energy, printing locally and choosing the materials we use carefully; we calculate our carbon footprint and doubly offset it through gold-standard schemes; and we plant a tree for every order we receive via our website to give back to the planet.

Find out more at:

RENARDPRESS.COM/ECO

About the poet

LJ is a vegan poet and bookseller from London. Her poems have been published by numerous journals, both in print and online, including *Green Ink Poetry*, *The Madrigal*, *Spellbinder Literary Magazine*, *Drawn to the Light*, *Acropolis Journal*, *Cerasus Magazine*, *Amphibian Literary Journal*, *Tiny Seed Journal*, *Black Bough*, *Spelt* and *Wild Greens*.

Her poetry features in the printed anthologies *Spectrum: Poetry Celebrating Identity* (Renard Press, 2022), *York Literary Review 2023* (Valley Press) and *Building Bridges* (Renard Press, 2024).

Her debut poetry collection, *Lessons from the Sky*, was published by Ellipsis Imprints in February 2024.